How

GREAT
B&B

from Zero to New York Times

Written by:

Sara Verrall

Title: How to Create a Great B&B
Sub-title: from Zero to New York Times

Author: Sara Verrall

Copyright © 2022 Sara Verrall

All rights reserved, including the right to reproduce this work- including photographs - in any form whatsoever, without permission in writing from the publisher, except for brief passages in connection with a review.

Publishers: Albatross Forlag Ltd
Address:
128 City Road, London EC1V 2NX ENGLAND

Author: Sara Verrall
Website: www.dreamitdoit.fr

Contact Data:
34340 Marseillan, Herault, Occitanie, FRANCE
e-mail: sara@dreamitdoit.fr

Rue Galilee B&B
website: www.ruegalilee.com

This book is available to order via Amazon.

Index of Contents

INTRODUCTION

Janne Larsson

Hello, my name is Janne.

My Swedish friends pronounce it "Yan" but I'm a friendly guy and am happy to answer to "Jan", "Yah'nee" or even "Jane" just so long as you are friendly too. If the second phrase is "Can I buy you a beer?" then you are already on the way to being a friend for life!

I am a professional electrician.

This is the best profession to get you through life, in my eyes … especially if you don't want to stay being "just" an electrician for all your days and nights.

Despite my laid-back exterior, in truth I'm not the type to stay still at all. I'm forever looking and researching; forever curious. And opportunities excite me.

My first job as an electrician, at seventeen years of age, was working on the very first North Sea oil platform "Mobil 1" in Stavanger Fjord in Norway. I then moved to work for over ten years in East Germany before the fall of The Wall. Thanks to these early experiences I learned to adapt and fit in with a team to get the job done. My one-year service in the Swedish Army drummed in the Musketeer's cry of "All for one and one for all" and

I hold true to that ethos, even today. However, despite this strong sense of team spirit, I am my own person, and I walk my own path.

As the years have progressed I have adapted and learnt to appreciate the strengths and qualities of others, as well as to acknowledge my own. This has given me the confidence and courage to follow through when I believe I am having a "really good idea".

With this book I hope to give you a bucketful of inspiration and some practical guidance, so that you too might take the leap to follow your own dream. There's a lot of joy and satisfaction to be had in creating and running your own B&B… but there can be pitfalls along the way. If this book helps you to avoid the worst, and to side-step a few more, then I'll be satisfied that these words were well-written and maybe I'll get to hear some of your tales of "How I did it", one day.

Before launching "Rue Galilee B&B" I had formed some pretty clear ideas about what worked, and what didn't, whenever I stayed as a guest in a hotel or at a B&B. As my plans crystalised and took shape, I knew I wanted to offer "The Best". Not the most prestigious, nor the most expensive, but the best attention to specific details to make sure that every guest's stay was enjoyable and memorable. I wanted everyone to come down to breakfast with a big smile on their face, to relax and chat at the Private Bar in the evenings, and to be impatient to visit us again. My aim was to offer "The Four Best B's" – not just two: the best beds, the best bathrooms, the best breakfast and the best bar.

Being a true Swede, blue-and-yellow to the core, my default belief is that the best of everything comes from Sweden. Since moving to France and experiencing the range of a truly international community, I do have to admit that sometimes The Best in a specific case might not necessarily be Swedish. You will find a list of my personal recommendation of best suppliers at the back of this book, which I hope will be useful … and you might notice that not all of them come from my home country. My mind has been opened. Feel free to make your own decisions; as you wish ~

One tale that might help you regarding your choice of beds, however, is the experience of a couple of early guests in my house who had journeyed from the North of France for their holidays. They freely admitted, weighing 130kg and 100kg respectively, that they were a heavier-than-average couple. The French-made bed in their previous night's guest house was not designed to take that weight. As they each went to lay down on their own side of the bed, it collapsed, folded in two and effectively imprisoned them! They were hooting with laughter the following night, enjoying a drink at my bar, as they told how their loud cries finally brought the host running. Fortunately, the Pompiers (firemen) summoned to their rescue did not need to bring in specialist lifting equipment … but it was a close call.

May I simply say that the best beds from Sweden, bearing the legendary name of Carpe Diem, would never have given up in that way. Which is why I have them in each room in my house. "No guest too heavy; no guest too tall" … so far!

So now I invite you to dive into these pages, to hear how I combined my passion to give The Best with my enthusiasm for meeting and making new friends; and how that dream comes true for me, every single day.

THE HOUSE TODAY

www.ruegalilee.com

CHAMBRES D' HÔTES
RUE GALILEE

CHAPTER 1.

HAVE A DREAM

Have a dream

We all have dreams; so many that we can't remember.

The dreams to follow are the ones that you dream just as vividly when you are awake as when you are asleep.

If you have a colourful, heartfelt dream that rings in your ears when the night skies are quiet; that interrupts your daydreams when the holidays are long; that simply refuses to be forgotten no matter how many years, fears and tears try to cloud your view ... that dream is A Keeper. You don't have to tell everyone your dream. In fact, I would advise that you really don't tell many people at all. So many will tell you that you're a fool. They will point out all the obvious obstacles, all the less-likely calamities that could crop up along the way, and then they will suggest a good few "far more sensible" paths for you to follow instead. They will never realise that for certain people (like you and I) any attempt at discouragement simply adds more fuel to the fire of our desires and we vow to push harder. For the sake of peace, try to nod, smile sweetly, then tell yourself they are only saying these things because they love you. … And keep dreaming anyway – but quietly!

Who can you tell?

Tell yourself. Often. Whenever you want to cheer yourself up. Whenever the present day seems too routine and regular, and you start to believe that you are stuck forever. We are never stuck forever. We don't have to "end up" anywhere. At least not until our final day has passed and there's a heap of earth and a heavy stone above us. And then you might be like me and believe that your spirit is still flying freely, anyway.

Tell one of the cheerleaders in your life. You will recognize them. They can come in many guises and may very well not be the people you might assume (or hope?) would cheer you on … but that's ok. We cannot designate roles for others in our lives. We can either welcome them as they are, or spend our days trying to change them to fit. For myself, I've generally been too busy focusing on my current path to try to drag others off theirs … with a few notable exceptions – but that could be another story, for another time.

To my heart's eternal joy, it was my father who

surprised me by rising up as a Chief Cheerleader on the two most significant occasions when others were taking me for a fool for dreaming so big.

My First Big Dream was to sail around the World, with just one friend, Carl, for company. After my father picked himself up off the floor from laughing – as Carl and I were both seasick electricians with not one hour's sailing experience between us at the time – it was he, and my brother, Anders, who took on running our family business for three years to set me free to do just that. There are two books, one in Swedish and one in English, that tell the tales of those three amazing years … so now it feels like it's about time I documented the path of my Second Big Dream.

It took me five years of preparation before I set off on my voyage around the World. My dream of owning a Bed & Breakfast had been in my mind for over twenty years before I took the first concrete steps to make that real. So don't despair if your dream is not happening yet. Hold on to your vision. Keep adding bits … and don't give up.

CHAPTER 2.

SORT THE FINANCE

Sort the finance

Any (legal) way that you can. It's very lovely and spiritual to have faith, "trust and the money will come", and other esoteric ideals. But if you can do your best to gather as much financial backing as you can, your life will be that much easier. You will never have enough money. Of course. We rarely have "enough" money – whether it's for buying a house, starting a family, or following any number of crazy dreams. That's part of the challenge.

If you've dreamt for long enough, you should be able to sketch on a piece of paper the key details of your plan to make it real. You don't have to be a financial wizard. There are other people who are that way inclined (see Chapter 7 about Asking for help). You just need to find a way to convey that you have a dream, you are awake, you have a good idea of what it will take (read on …) and you are prepared to do it.

Do your research. There are so many aspects and expenses associated with starting a business – in any country. As a Swede moving to France the official legislation was daunting, not to mention the cost of translations! I was blessed very early on to form a terrific friendship with an Italian/French guy called Roberto who had just gone through so many of the same processes to open his own B&B in town. He and his lovely wife Peggy patiently guided me through the seemingly endless forms and paperwork. They gently laughed as I exclaimed at "yet another Tax"; all of which were essential and totally unavoidable. Running a B&B in a country where you can actually speak the language would obviously have been a far easier choice – but that's the thing about following dreams. Heart choices are not often logical, but they are invariably good!

Fortunately, I have a very good Connection in the Swedish bank that my father had been with for many years. This person has watched both he, my brother and I as we've conducted ourselves in life and businesses over the years, so he understood and accepted my request for the rather large loan necessary to get this thing started. The Connection at the bank had been around long enough to appreciate that we have to call the first three years of any new enterprise

"The Dog Years"; when we work like dogs for very little return. We've all heard the term "speculate to accumulate". To truly speculate on a grand scale we invest our hearts and souls, and often hard physical labour, just as much as we invest the money. It's all part of making a dream happen.

The other benefit to sorting the finances is that it gives a shape to the next steps along the way.

CHAPTER 3.

KNOW WHAT YOU WANT

Know what you want

> Know what you want.
>> Know what you want.
>>> Know what you want.

It's great to be open-minded to other suggestions and ideas. I benefitted hugely from well-qualified professionals who had expert experience in relevant fields. I also benefitted from a few crazy contacts who had wacky ideas that I really loved and could incorporate into my overall plan. But that was the important fact. It was my overall plan. I knew what I wanted; how I wanted it to be and how I wanted it to feel when we welcomed our first guests. I knew how hard I was prepared to work in the beginning, and how hard I would need to work in the future. That didn't put me off.

If your dream doesn't make your eyes shine and you don't leap out of bed in the morning, eager to start another day in your own Personal Paradise … then perhaps you are not living the dream of your dreams.

If you're the type of person who struggles to choose when given too many options, then perhaps you're not ready to go-it-alone just yet. My current partner's business mentor once told her "Any decision is better than no decision". There's wisdom in those words. Once you have decided, it is possible to pour your energy into making "it" work no matter what comes next. I believe that we only have one life (this time around) so why not make sure that the decision you take is the best one for you. Absolutely.

Dreaming can be dangerous. It can cause chaos in many families and relationships because we are not always all on the same page at the same time. This can be hard. You alone can work out what your priorities are. I can only hope, for you, that the ones you love will either choose to jump into your dream with equal enthusiasm; joyfully join you from time to time when their chosen dream allows; or let you go with love. There are many shades of grey to these scenarios, of course. Have courage. Be yourself. Who else can you be?

In hindsight, I can now see that I convinced my ex-wife that owning and running a B&B would be a brilliant way for us to have a great life, as well as providing a reasonable income to take us beyond conventional retirement years.

Unfortunately, despite her early involvement, it became evident that we no longer shared the same dreams, and we parted company less than one year after we opened the doors of our exciting new project.

As I said, dreams can cause chaos and some relationships simply cannot withstand the changes and uncertainty of chaotic times. All we can do is stay honest, try to communicate, try to be kind, and wish each other well ... whichever route we choose to follow.

CHAMBRES D' HÔTES
RUE GALILEE

CHAPTER 4.

FIND THE HOUSE

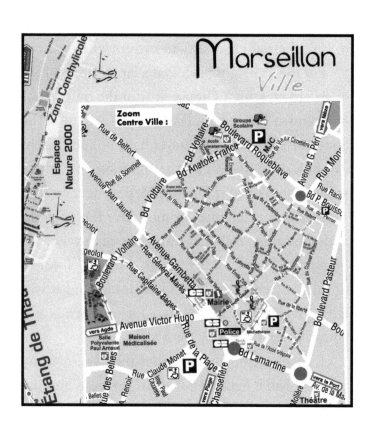

Find the house

If you are wanting to create a B&B you will need to find the right property to inspire you.

For me, the right place was a large, almost-ruin of an old merchant's house, lost in the quiet heart of old town Marseillan. If you had asked me, "The South of France" would never have popped out of my mouth in answer to the question "So where would you like your Dream B&B to be located?"

Please don't get me wrong. I love the warmth, and the wine, and the ambience of my chosen home … but I didn't speak French, I knew nothing of French laws and customs, and it was a long way – over 2000kms – for my friends and countrymen to pop by for a visit.

I wasn't seeing any obstacles the day I met my house. I had a lightning flash in my head and my heart screamed "This is it!!" It was like hitting the jackpot on a pinball machine. My Dad, who was out strolling with me, did ask "Are you sure?" which was more restrained than the Estate Agent's incredulous "What???" when he opened the door for me and all I could say was "Wow!". The agent had spent four years opening that door and pretty-much actively restraining the (potential) clients from bolting straight out again … my enthusiasm took him completely by surprise.

Unless you are a professional builder or architect, you will be well-advised to hunt around and find the best of these professionals to help you. Nearly all of us can have ideas of how to decorate a house; not many of us have skills and experience to make the best use of space, and to build a place that feels like it can stand the tests of time. I had worked with a brilliant commercial architect in Sweden on many occasions and admired his work in restaurants, shops and other business premises. He really is top in his field. We have an ease of communication, built on years of practical co-operation. When I called David, he could immediately follow my descriptions of the treasure I felt I had unearthed. The reassurance of him practically screaming "Buy it! Buy it!" down the phone line was all I needed. My French stone-mason friend, Khalid, had already confirmed that the key structural bits were firmly enough in place; after standing nearly four hundred years already the house was not going fall down any time soon. I just had to check one final detail, with my electrician's head firmly in place: did the house have the three-phase wiring necessary to support commercial-sized activities? "Yes". So I bought it.

Having found your house, give it a name. Preferably one that is short and easy to remember. You are going to have a deep and lasting relationship with this property; it needs to assume an identity and status of its own. If you do everything right, your guests might well fall in love with the property too. So, it needs a name ~

If you possibly can, find out any stories and back-history surrounding your new-found home and the surrounding location. Guests love to hear details that add memorable colour to their stay. Obviously, this is easier if you have taken on an older property. Not only do we have a deep well in the internal courtyard at Rue Galilee that impresses small children and learned historians in equal measure, but we also found a small stone font in the cupboard at the side of the Bar. We can genuinely say that we feel blessed to live here, although we offer a different kind of spiritual refreshment to visitors nowadays!

That cupboard also used to house The Telephone when this was the first house in town to be connected to the early-days communications network. So perhaps it is hardly surprising that the friendly "drop-in" atmosphere all callers feel exists; there's been a warm welcome at Rue Galilee for longer than we appreciate, I think.

If you cannot claim any particular treasures unique to your house, you don't necessarily have to let that stop you! I once followed a host from another B&B, in another part of France, as she led a group of visitors around her village late one evening. With wine glass in hand, she regaled her guests with tales of "Saint Marie performed a miracle here ..." and "This is where they discovered some dinosaur bones in the 1960's ..." and "There's a legend of two star-crossed lovers from opposing families, one who lived just over the river ..." At a convenient pause I took her to one side and expressed my astonishment at so much history being connected to such a small, tucked-away town. With a giggle she confided that "perhaps not *all* the stories are attached to this *exact* location, but they are true tales I heard around the region ... and my guests are loving it!"

I'll leave that up to you and your conscience. In these internet days of Google & Co. it could prove simpler to dig a little deeper and find a few solid facts, but – in truth – her guests were loving it.

CHAPTER 5.

MAKE
CONNECTIONS

Make connections

It helps if you are the friendly type. Unless you want to run a B&B in the style of Basil Fawlty in the universally known and much-quoted British TV series "Fawlty Towers".

Swedish people are, in my opinion, mostly friendly and open. We don't put curtains or shutters across our windows; we like to connect with people in our neighbourhood.

Moving to a new town, in a new country, we needed to get to know everything about how to fit in and make our lives work. Not just for the business, but socially too. That's a day-by-day process. You can work out, by a process of elimination, which is the best bakery in town for your daily baguettes and croissants. But you cannot force the pace of friendships. Show up, be genuine, and put a smile on your face as you get stuck in to each day's new adventure. Regardless of the size of your project, you will be so busy investigating, planning, fixing and doing that you won't have time to contemplate or worry about what everyone thinks of the New Kid in Town, anyway. Just keep on going and keep on smiling.

One of my favourite ice-breakers was honouring the tradition of the Friday After Work Club. Taking out stones from a dividing wall and setting them to one side created the foundations for our future Private Bar in the B&B ... and coincidentally set up the perfect spot to share a beer, or two, on Fridays. Relaxing together after shared endeavours creates a special bond. Whether it was with the guys who had worked beside me all week, or with friends who had just stopped by to see how it was all going and ended up getting their hands dirty for an hour or two (or more). I was blessed with a steady stream of friendly faces, and formed some great friendships in those early, exhausting months. Friends come and go throughout our lives, for a variety of reasons, but it is truly heart-warming feeling to raise a glass today with those who laid the first stones, lifter the first buckets and drank the first beers in that dusty worksite!

Do everything you can to get on with your neighbours. In Old Town Marseillan my neighbours have been living in their tightly-packed, characterful houses for years, if not generations. They are well-established and I recognised that I was causing a disruption to their peaceful home environment. It was a major disruption, too – with noise and dust pretty much every day for ten months, as I worked to achieve the opening-date deadline I had set myself. I might not have been able to speak their language, but I nodded and smiled and did a few of my "expressive mimes" to attempt to convey how grateful I was that they tolerated the mess I was making on their doorstep.

To be fair, I think we gave them great entertainment too. They knew the house; it had been standing empty for some time and I think they appreciated that I was bringing life and colour back to its faded walls. It might have been a bit embarrassing sometimes when they witnessed a few of my silly mistakes as I learnt a whole set of new trade skills … but usually I could laugh with them. It was important for me to be on site every day, even if I wasn't always doing the most important jobs. I could carry buckets, drive to the tip, or nip and pick up extra supplies – of materials or snacks – as necessary. If you are not physically present, there is always the possibility that even the best of workers might get distracted … I think you know what I'm saying.

If your new neighbours want to be curious and have a look around – let them in and take the time to explain your vision! They might tell their friends and family that you are working hard to create a place for them to come and stay one day. It doesn't matter if you lose some working time this way. My neighbours have become warm friends, who also keep an eye on my home, take delivery of my post, and observe with fond amusement the international visitors the house now brings to their street.

Word-of-mouth was the cause of one especially joyful and emotional event in our new home. Somebody heard that the old house had been lovingly awakened, and they immediately chose it for a very special reunion. A local French man had met a beautiful Dutch girl on Marseillan beach when they were both students. They had a summer romance, then separated and got on with their lives in their different countries. Thirty years of marriages, children and divorces later, they found each other again – thanks to the wonders of the internet. They met and the spark was re-ignited. They gathered their families together to witness their exchange of loving vows in the church at Marseillan. And why did they choose Rue Galilee as the ideal location for the wedding feast? Because the groom remembered the house where his father had played as a small boy! We all shed many happy tears that afternoon, as the elderly gentleman walked from room to room, exclaiming in delight to see we had kept and restored the original craftsmen's details all around the house. The families have created a new set of happy memories now, and they plan to return and revisit us soon. And so the memory-making goes on …

We are fortunate that the South of France climate means we can dine outside, at the little tables at the front of the house, for many months of the year. This might not be possible so often for you, if you choose a Northern European country to make your home. But I urge you to be outside as much as you can. Cleaning the car, cutting the hedges, fixing whatever … make yourself accessible for casual conversations. Day-to-day life can revolve much easier with the regular lubrication of a five-minute chat about the simple things. Then if something big crops up, and you need the human connection, you will find that you are already part of a natural social network … which leads to my next bit of advice:

CHAMBRES D' HÔTES
RUE GALILEE

CHAPTER 6.

HELP OTHERS

Help others

My girlfriend, Sara, is writing this book and she tells me I have to mention here that you must learn when to say "No". She might be right – sometimes – but please don't tell her I said so!

I love helping other people. It makes me happy. I am also an "instant fixer" sort of man. If I can see how to solve a problem, or how to get a job done, then why not "do it now"? The thing is, with a five-bedroom Bed & Breakfast to run I have to wear a lot of different hats every day, so I don't always have that many minutes left in any twenty-four-hour period.

You might want to prepare yourself for this List of Hats if you are still reading and are as keen as ever to follow your dream. At different times, and sometimes simultaneously, you will need to be:

Breakfast Chef

Friendly chatty Host when serving breakfast

Bookings, check-in and check-out Clerk

Chief (only) table-clearer and washer-upper

Cleaner of all bedrooms, toilets, dining salon, kitchen and courtyard

Laundryman. Wash, dry and fold. Everything.

Ironing Maestro! With my Italian ironing board and Swedish dance-band music I get in the groove and drive that Ferrari down country lanes (in my imaginings!)

Welcoming Host and house-tour Guide

Tourism information source for beaches, restaurants, vineyards, markets, etc.

Bicycle repairman. Always keep a good supply of puncture repair kits in house.

Bar tender; keeping the bar well stocked - gin, tonic, ice(!) and plenty of beer and wine - and keeping our guests well "watered". And of course you need to be a very good listener, with just a few stories of your own to tell.

Boss of Multi-media promotions. Nowadays Sara takes responsibility for most of the marketing and promotional side of the business, but I still play a very active role in the technical and administrative side of things. I was rather forcefully advised, when attending the required five-day business management course, to "Never employ anybody in France!" Apparently, the employment laws are structured so firmly in the employee's favour that it is almost impossible to fire someone, no matter how bad they might be! The employment laws could be different in your country, but this is something I strongly advise you to investigate if you plan to build a team to work alongside you. Fortunately, Sara had already established her self-employed status in France so we can operate our separate businesses in harmony, but independently.

There are always more tasks than hours in the day, but working from six o'clock in the morning until midnight for those hot, High Season months clouds my memory. I could possibly have omitted a few hats from the above list.

Consequently, if I am asked to fix a broken shelf, adapt a faulty light fitting, or rescue a cat from a balcony whilst sitting outside at my Office sharing a healthy, tasty, home-cooked dinner with my girlfriend … well, I think you can understand why she doesn't always smile quite so brightly, and has been known to ask "Can it wait?" Helping others is great, but if we can choose a time when I do, in fact, have a free moment or two it is a lot nicer for everyone!

One other piece of advice that springs to mind, especially if you intend to be The Handyman on your project and to be actively involved installing the electrical appliances, fixing the leaky plumbing etcetera is "For Goodness Sake - write it down!" If any of us are hit by that mythical bus which is threatened throughout our lives, it would certainly help those that follow to at least have a rough sketch idea of how things work. When you are working on site, making and fixing and doing, you are invariably too busy to make copious reems of notes. But in the quiet moments, before your little grey cells get too tired, you might just want to record some of the bigger details. It's a sobering thought, I know, but none of us know what's around the corner. It could be The Golden Jackpot; it could be that pesky bus. "Enough said" I think ~

CHAMBRES D'HÔTES
RUE GALILEE

CHAPTER 7.

ASK FOR HELP

Ask for help

You cannot be The Expert at everything. Yes, it's your dream and you are following your own script. You can pick up new skills, for sure, but try to acknowledge the areas where you have less strength and then do your best to find really nice people who are willing to help. Then don't just rely on their niceness; be prepared to pay them – fairly, and well. They are making the difference between whether your dream succeeds or fails; fair payment is the minimum recognition for their contribution.

I have already briefly mentioned two of the three key contributors to my dream's success in the sections above. Roberto and Peggy gave me the foundation of their knowledge for running my B&B and we still regularly turn to each other for help and encouragement. We have our own houses, but as Hosts we are colleagues in welcoming tourists to Marseillan. Khalid is a master craftsman who learnt his trade in Paris before choosing the warmth of the South as a more natural climate for his Moroccan roots. He works with respect for the stones and tiles of his craft, and the care with which he treats these organic materials is reflected in the results he achieves. I have learnt a great deal, working beside him, not to mention those choice French swear words, too! Khalid's son-in-law, Roman, was the awesomely cheerful powerhouse of strength, working beside us in that dusty house as we crafted its transformation. His skills are akin to those of his father-in-law, and his boundless energy was a welcome boost when us two older chaps were occasionally flagging at the end of the day. He added another couple of words to my "French building site" vocabulary, which I won't repeat here out of respect for your delicate ears!

The other hugely significant person is Manuela, who not only is an effortless translator between French, German and English, but she is also someone who speaks from her soul and has brought light to my days in endless ways. We refer to her as The Angel of Marseillan as she glides around town on her bicycle, laden with useful things, always on her way to "just lend a hand" to someone in the neighbourhood. She does way more than just lend a hand; she seeks, and then finds, whatever each person needs … but she takes little personal credit for it. We are all richer for her presence, her presents and her smiles.

There have been many, many others along the way and I have always done my best to repay their help with food, drinks or by simply "returning the favour". There is another much-repeated truism that "A friend comes into your life for a reason, a season or a lifetime". I believe it's a sign that you are on the right path and "in the flow" when people show up at exactly the right moment, with exactly the advice or skill you need, right there and then.

There was a guy called Nik who did just that. He presented himself at my door asking if I needed a carpenter to help with the works in progress. "Yes please", that would be very helpful … but as I was showing him around the house and pointing out all the jobs he could tackle, I could see the colour draining from his face. "You're not a carpenter" was the only observation I could make. "What can you do?" Nik told me he wanted to work, but he wasn't sure if I could use his primary skill as a sign-writer. I most definitely could! He's an incredible artist, sign writer and all-round precision worker and talented man! Not only has he written the names of all five rooms above their respective doors, but he's also crafted a beautiful Rue Galilee hanging street sign and designed a fabulous logo for our House Champagne bottles. Knowing I can call on his skills lets my mind wander to new creative enterprises from time to time. I am currently nurturing an idea featuring a Swedish moose which I'm sure he will interpret; our happy association is a win/win for both of us!

Another example of "right timing" for me was when I had some very prestigious house guests who were responsible for a globally-renowned luxury hotel chain. They loved everything I had built at Rue Galilee but they candidly informed me that my website was "Sh*t". I could not thank them enough! In my heart I knew that my attempts at writing all that promotional blurb really showed up my limitations when messing about with written words. It's ok – charming even – to muddle through with "Sw-inglish" when chatting face-to-face …but so much can get lost in translation, and frequently did!

A long-time friend and professional photographer, in Sweden, instantly sprang to mind as the guy I needed to capture the essence of the house. The offer of a week's holiday for himself and his family was the extra carrot I could offer to enhance the mates-rates fee he volunteered to do the job. What a bonus! I got to spend a fun week together with those lovely people and now have the most incredible portfolio of images of my house, the bar and salon; taken at prime hours over the days to truly capture the atmosphere. Never under-estimate the value of warmth and friendship; it can add a deep lustrous colour to any piece of work.

And as for romance: the re-writing of my website, and subsequent marketing work, is what lead to the relationship I now have with my girlfriend. Following the amused recommendation of a couple of friends from her old village, she knocked on my door when she first moved into town and announced "They told me you were friendly". I can be. Our first coffee and chat established that she enjoyed writing and she was enthusiastic to help promote all that I love about this house. A lot of words and a lot of work later … and here we are today.

One other couple I must mention who came across my doorstep in a less-than-conventional way are Anna and Adam. Anna's father was a businessman who wanted to provide a luxury location for his daughter and her wedding guests. He and his wife stayed with us at Rue Galilee before and after the main event, so his daughter was regularly popping in to discuss last minute details with her mother. The wedding ceremony and celebrations took place in grand style at a nearby Chateau. Afterwards, Anna and Adam moved into a little house just along the road, then came knocking to ask if they might jump onto my internet for their work as they were not yet connected at their new home. "Of course". As a thank you for the quiet working space and endless cups of coffee they asked if they could help me in any way. It turned out that they understand the internal workings of Google and its advertising algorithms ... so now Rue Galilee is most professionally promoted on this very important platform. Thank you so much.

Overall, you are going to create your home and business in your own way, to reflect your personal style and values. I just urge you to remain open to input coming from other sources too. There are people who might shine a light from a different angle that compliments your vision perfectly, in ways previously unimagined.

CHAPTER 8.

FOLLOW THE
RULES

Follow the rules

You might have "the rebel instinct". It sometimes goes with the territory when you're a risk taker. But be sensible here. Even if you're not operating in a foreign land with complex rules detailed in lengthy foreign documents – trust me! You are starting a venture in The Public Eye; you will be under the gaze of curious eyes ... and not everyone is as friendly as we might hope. Some people don't enjoy seeing others succeed. Some people resent changes inflicted on their home environment if they are not consulted first. Some people are just bored and have nothing better to do than check up on you.

Life is much easier if you toe the line and follow the rules. You can sleep soundly at night, and you don't have to be constantly on your guard to remember what you might have told to who, and what you don't want to tell him, or her. I welcome a huge variety of people to my house and to the private bar in the evenings. My biggest confession is that I don't always remember everybody's name all the time. If I had to add "being deceitful" to my social interactions, I think I would crack up!

One thing I wanted to do was to construct a mini terrace at the front of my house. With Roberto by my side we went to the Mairie (town hall) to ask advice and fill in the necessary application. The following day not only did the technical specialists for Road Construction and Furnishings arrive outside the house, but also the Pompiers (firemen) and the Police Municipale! There was a healthy amount of French-style discussion, which was as intense, and time consuming, as the assessment of rival boules placements around the "cochon" (target ball) at any friendly contest, in any town, on any day. Angles were checked, measurements taken and re-checked ... and finally the official parameters of my proposed little patch were agreed. The Chief of the assessment team then produced a can of white spray paint and formalized the outline. It was not the same configuration as a scene-of-crime shape, thankfully, but it certainly carried the same gravitas.

This outside space is just big enough to take two tables and four chairs. It is fondly known of as my Office, as I can be found there at all times of day and night; whenever I get the chance, really. The fact that it is on the corner angle of my house is what provoked such fiercely focused scrutiny from all concerned; you need every last millimetre when navigating these narrow streets in a modern car. And, sure enough, a nosey neighbour was provoked to demand "Have you got permission for that?" the moment she saw me place the first slice of decking. She even summoned the Police Municipale – just in case! I admit it was quietly satisfying, as well as a big relief, to be able to prove that "Yes" all the i's had been dotted and all the t's had been crossed.

If you show you are doing your best to comply with all the regulations, you are more likely to be forgiven, and excused for being a foreigner, if you occasionally fail to fill in the correct piece of paperwork at the correct moment. Each year the Police Municipale call by to remind me that I need to renew the Permit so that my terrace can remain in place. They know that the annual payment will be made without hesitation. No hassle. That's the way I want to live my life.

It pays to be mindful of the less formal but equally important social rules too. We love to have late evenings at The Bar, especially when an international mix of guests provokes some stimulating conversations. We were all reduced to tears of laughter the evening a Swiss guest explained, in great detail but with wonky English skills, that you really had to take "pot luck" when shooting ducks for dinner, as you could never tell until after the event the true number of flight miles that duck might have flown! There was another uproarious occasion when a neighbour's brother threatened to "go the whole way" in a mock striptease routine to entertain a group of girls visiting from Sweden! Fortunately, he was more talk than trousers, and he kept his hat on, but be reminded, keep your motto: "Be Prepared". Anything can happen when you install a gyrating mirrored disco-ball and a party-level sound system, with optional karaoke ~ If you've also installed a high level of sound proofing between the floors and invested in top quality double-glazed windows, then everybody can stay happy and nobody is disturbed. You might not get the ideal amount of sleep that night, but parties don't happen every day and the memories will last forever.

CHAPTER 9.

BE GENEROUS

Be generous

Every penny counts, of course, and you will always need to have an eye on balancing the books; doing all you can to ensure that enough comes in to cover what needs to be paid out. But there are plenty of ways of being generous with the "smaller stuff". Little gestures can add that extra shine to your guests' holiday which mean you and your B&B will be remembered with a warm smile. Give a choice of three jams for breakfast, not just one. Give a glass of water to passers-by on a hot day, when they are lost and tired in the labyrinth of narrow streets of the old town. Offer a slice of watermelon when a friend passes by your street-table, as you take a shaded moment to refresh your own energy, before carrying on with the jobs of the day.

Put more cushions on the bed than are strictly necessary. You never know when someone might need that extra comfort.

Choose the higher quality bed linen and towels. This will be a good economic decision as well as giving a more luxurious feel; quality lasts.

Top quality bed linen and towels can withstand the higher temperatures required to ensure guaranteed cleanliness at every wash.

A couple of friends who have just opened their own B&B in our town are offering a pre-dinner, complimentary glass of wine beside their swimming pool each evening. We think this is a genuinely nice gesture, telling their guests that they are truly welcome in their home.

Whatever you decide to offer, be sure you can offer it freely, consistently, and with an open heart. If you over-stretch yourself, wishing to create an outstanding initial impression, you might come to resent that extravagant gesture as time passes. It's better to under-promise and over-deliver; then everyone continues to feel good about it.

You can be charming, but you don't have to be over-generous to everyone. You will easily recognize those people who are wanting to take more; to have "something for nothing". Genuine guests appreciate that you are taking extra care, making extra effort ... and even if they don't "reward" your generosity with extra purchases, don't worry. They will give you their "pay back" later, by singing your praises far and wide as they move on with their journey.

As someone who habitually loves to give that little bit extra, it is possible that I have sometimes given out more enthusiastically than wisely. My best solution to this most human error is not to keep count! Others have been more incredibly generous to me than I can ever repay; on the Grand Scales of Life it all comes right in the end …

One final point; always remember to be generous to yourself as well. You are working hard, taking risks and achieving new highs in unfamiliar tasks. At the start of your project you will have made a list, or many lists, of everything you need to achieve. Stop regularly, look back at the path and notice how far you've already come. Relish each time you can tick something off those lists, and make sure you pat yourself vigorously on the back and say "Well done!" And don't just have a beer; have champagne! You've earned it. Nobody else knows to what extent you have pushed yourself along the way; nobody else is going to praise you with such awareness of every detail. You are the one doing all of this, and you need to be your own best cheerleader, too!

CHAPTER 10.

LEARN THE LINGO

Learn the lingo

What can I say?

As a Swede, I can usually understand and be understood in Danish and Norwegian as well as by my countrymen, although my southern accent has challenged a few ⁓. I learned basic English at school and have brushed up on that in recent years as I have to admit – reluctantly – that English is probably one of the most useful global languages. But French? It just did not sit naturally in my ears from Day One. By the time it reached my brain there was very little for my stunned grey cells to work with.

Never one to quit, I have got-by in France, speaking next-to-no French, for eight years now. Obviously, I owe an enormous debt of gratitude to those key players who worked with me and translated the mountains of necessary, most-confusing paperwork that is part of every business. My builder friend, Khalid, taught me to recognize the products in our local "Brico" (D.I.Y.) stores, as well as how to swear regularly and emphatically in perfect French ("Merde!")

My great friends, Roberto and Peggy, can always be relied upon to interpret and explain all the confusing correspondence I receive about the house. And with the help of the miracle that is Manuela (who can hear one language, immediately convert it and speak another) we took, between us, two intensive, five-day, hotel licensing courses. She heard in French, spoke to me in German, and I took notes in Swedish. Reverse the process, pass the tests and shake your head!

I have found my rusty language skills often give my guests more confidence to "have a go" as we both look for common-ground and common-understanding in our second languages. We share the joke that I'm fluent in Swedish, they are fluent in French, and we are both muddling along, as best we can, in English. With the willingness to mime the odd frustratingly elusive essential word, we find our way.

Recently, for a brief period - when most of the town-centre restaurants were closed - I was offering my house guests an evening meal menu of three choices. Waggling hand (fish) flapping elbows (chicken) or fingers making horns on my head and "Moo!" conveyed the options perfectly.

"How would you like that cooked?" required more hand mimes and sizzle-sounds. My cooking has consistently received rave reviews. Don't ever let a lack of words fail you!

It has helped enormously that my English girlfriend applied herself more vigorously to learning French than I did, during her first four years living in France (before she met me). To be fair, she wasn't spending those four years renovating a ruin and setting up a B&B, but she was carving her own unique path in this foreign land and her commitment to learning and speaking is awesome. She was not at all confident the first time she took a customer's credit card details over the telephone, to reserve a booking for that weekend – but she did it! She's taken many more bookings since, which has been a fundamental improvement to the success rate of our telephone reservations system. She tells me that each nationality delivers sets of numbers in their own format. French people tend to prefer numbers in blocks-of-two … so that instead of saying "three" then "four" when giving the first digits of our postcode we say "thirty-four" – which at the same time conveys the number of our Department. The blocks-of-two format doesn't always hold fast however, as the final three digits of the post code are expressed as "three hundred and forty" … but I think you get my drift. It's worth learning, because if you express your phone number in blocks-of-three format, or any other mixture, you might as well be speaking Double-Dutch! The numbers simply will not compute in French ears ⁓

CHAPTER 11.

ADAPT. BE FLEXIBLE

Adapt. Be flexible

You might think that you know exactly how things will work, but in truth plans don't always go according to plan. You can fight against it, or you can adapt and try to find a new way. Sometimes, the new way will work better than the original way; sometimes it won't – but "Whatever"; staying flexible is a healthy mental approach as well as good for the body!

A major challenge presented itself very soon after we opened the doors of our new business. The commercial laundry service, located in the nearby town of Agde, just could not keep up with the demands from the surrounding hotels and restaurants. Driving backwards and forwards, on busy roads in the summer heat, created an unacceptable daily stress in our lives. It wasn't the fault of the laundry management or staff; they were as helpful and willing as possible ... there was just too much work for them to keep on top of.

To me, the solution had to be to create my own laundry within our building. I sourced a commercial-scale washing machine that could take in hot water, rather than heat it as part of the process, so that I could do all my washing at optimum temperatures – but in fifty-five minutes per load rather than three hours. With a big, efficient drier and solar panels on the roof to provide the hot water – and my "Ferrari" ironing board (as already mentioned) - I was back in control, with a calmer blood pressure reading too!

You need to be willing to spend a large part of your "B&B Host" life in the laundry. You will wash, dry, fold and iron more fabric than you can ever imagine, so set up your laundry room so you can work as comfortably as possible. I have even slept in my primary workspace for a night when my original, unreliable booking system lost track and sold the same room twice, so that I had to give up my apartment when weary guests arrived. Being flexible feels far better than disappointing someone on their annual holiday. It was just for one night, and I was so tired that the little camp-bed beneath the hanging, drying sheets felt both cosy and comfortable.

You need to stay flexible about the bigger plans as well as the smaller details. I certainly didn't anticipate that I would be running this business on my own, but when my marriage ended I wanted even more fervently to succeed with my dream; it was the best lifestyle to carry me through to the end of my days – I was sure of that.

As luck would have it, a younger Swedish couple arrived to save me from some long, lonely winter's evenings. Jesper and Christina had been searching across the region for a place to start their own B&B, but had not found anywhere suitable that was within their budget. They only intended to stay one night with me before resuming their search, but they had arrived after the harbour-front restaurants had closed for the evening and they were hungry. I said they were welcome to share a meal with me and Jesper offered to help me with the food preparation. Just a couple of seconds of watching that man wield a knife told me he was no stranger in a kitchen! He was, in fact, a renowned chef in my home country… and he was looking for work in France.

Our conversation that dinnertime, sharing food and wine in the best, friendliest tradition, led to us establishing a working arrangement that benefited us all. Jesper and Christina formed their own restaurant company, called La Place, rented my kitchen, and served meals in the dining room at Rue Galilee. I helped as an extra pair of hands if necessary and served drinks from the in-house private bar. It had been part of my future ambition to run a restaurant in the house … and here it was happening much sooner than I expected. Yes, it was a different business set-up than I had in mind, but it worked perfectly for all of us and I really enjoyed their company. I was sad when they ultimately decided to return to Sweden in 2020 to follow their dream of having a B&B of their own, but we have stayed in contact and they visited us in Marseillan just a couple of months ago. I was flattered to hear that they had implemented a few of my ideas in the house they have created to welcome their own guests. In actual fact, their enthusiasm to replicate the best of Rue Galilee was part of the push to write this book.

CHAPTER 12.

SMILE

Smile

If you cannot say "Of course" with genuine enthusiasm and warmth, to whatever requests your guests make, then you need to leave the house.

If you cannot open the door and greet everyone with the human-equivalent of Labrador-puppy enthusiasm, then perhaps hosting is not the role for you.

Everyone can smell a fake. And who wants to be a fake in their own life anyway? You simply cannot pretend to be happy to meet and talk with someone if it isn't true. I believe that everybody has an interesting story to tell, if you are willing to listen for long enough. As a host, you need to make time. The strangers you meet today can become friends that you will welcome back tomorrow.

A major motivation for my voyage around the World was the chance to meet a variety of interesting people. Now an endless variety of interesting people come to my house in Marseillan every day. How lucky am I?

It's not difficult to smile if you feel this way. I hope you find encouragement in these pages to make your dream of owning a Bed & Breakfast come true, too. It is a big leap, and a lot of hard work, and it doesn't suit everybody, but if you have the passion for it then give it a go …

… Why not?

It's great to see Jesper and Christina making a success of their enterprise in Sweden, although I did have to remind Jesper when he visited "It's all about the people" and that he has to talk with his guests now! When he cooked his delicious dinners at La Place at Rue Galilee he preferred to stay in the kitchen and had said, more than once, "I prefer animals to humans". He tended to escape at the end of the evening to take his cat for a walk, leaving Christina to explain the details of the menu, and she and I to be the sociable hosts as we served one final drink at the bar. He tells me he has mellowed and is really enjoying conversations round the table in his new house. Well done, my friend!

However, for all of us there comes a time when you need to:

CHAMBRES D' HÔTES
RUE GALILEE

CHAPTER 13.

STAND BACK AND CHECK ...

Stand back and check ...

Ask yourself "Is this still my dream?"

It is easy to get so busy on the hamster-wheel of self-employment that we spend all our waking hours, and some of our sleeping ones, just keeping on top of everything; not taking any time-out to think or re-think this major aspect of our life's plan.

I do not intend to be insensitive, but - in truth - the total halt enforced across France at the beginning of the health crisis in 2020 gave me a chance to stop and take a clear-eyed look at how I was running my business. What was immediately apparent was that I'd been running myself ragged, trying to accommodate everyone who called, regardless of the strain it placed on me and how it sometimes inconvenienced my partner. Giving up my apartment and sleeping in the laundry room in the height of summer is an amusing anecdote but not a situation to be repeated too often. That incident prompted me to investigate an alternative, fail-safe, computerized booking system called Elloha, which was invented by a French company. It is a brilliant platform for managing your website, and for controlling not only the room bookings but also the add-on services you might want to offer. I bought ten bicycles specifically for hiring out to guests which can be pre-reserved when arranging their stay. If guests have a late arrival time we can offer them a light bar snack when they finally get here; again, this is bookable in advance. I have been delighted with Elloha from the first moment I switched systems. In addition, their updates and analyses are valuable extras, freely given in the spirit of "delivering more" that I most admire. In this instance there was a silver lining to that double-booking mini-drama, but it is not how we really want to make business decisions.

The other major change the 2020 chaos brought was to finally hold fast to a decision we had discussed but never implemented. We stopped taking One Night Only bookings. When you are building a reputation, and getting your hospitality business off the ground, then you have to offer One Night Only stays. When you have five rooms to clean and make presentable, and five sets of laundry to wash and iron, the daily pressure mounts relentlessly. If a friend stops by for a beer and a chat, that's at least an hour you've lost and cannot get back. I love to stop and chat, but I hate the stress of seeing a pile of sheets and towels waiting to be processed. With the additional level of cleaning required to fulfill safety standards against cross-infection, the one-night stay became impossible. And the benefits are enormous! Not only is there a far better chance that not all of my guests will check out on the same day, but now – most happily – we have more time to chat and get to know each on a deeper level. For sure, it is possible to connect with someone within minutes of their arrival, and I've enjoyed some deep belly-laughs with friends who were strangers an hour before. But, in general, the more time you spend with someone the richer the connection can become.

Fortunately, I had been running my Bed & Breakfast business for over three years before the lockdowns were brought in; I had built my reputation, I had repeat visitors, and I had even achieved a glowing commendation from a New York Times journalist. He described my house as "one of the most delightful small hotels I've ever found in France". It brought about my "Empire State moment" of website views statistics, as the number of clicks the day after the article jumped to over two thousand instead of the usual daily average of a couple of hundred. I am very, very proud of that, and the full review is framed and hanging on the wall in our reception area. Unfortunately, the lockdown that came six months later rather negated that incredible free publicity, but now that travel is opening up again we are benefiting from those earlier years, and Rue Galilee's profile in the USA is gently climbing. I can - at last - keep to my Three Nights Minimum Stay policy, attract enough guests to pay the bills, and continue to enjoy this hosting lifestyle.

You can see, from all the above, that my path has not always unfolded as originally intended. I don't doubt that there will be other bumps along the way. That's life. We can either sit down and complain or keep ourselves open to the new route that inevitably follows.

There will be one other personal decision, however, that we all must face - one day:

CHAPTER 14.

KNOW WHEN TO STOP

Know when to stop

When you can no longer open the door, excited to welcome whoever is standing on the other side, being a host is no longer the role for you.

After more than six years of running Rue Galilee B&B my enthusiasm has not shrunk one bit. I leap out of bed every morning proclaiming "Welcome to another day in Paradise" and I really mean it. I am living my dream and loving every minute of it. As I've already said: sailing around the World took me to meet so many different people; now they come to me!

You will find me happily dancing in the kitchen as I prepare the breakfasts, with a smile on my face and a song in my heart. My schoolteacher told me, many years ago, that "singing is not for you" so it's probably best that the songs are performed by the legions of artists on my Spotify playlists, and not by this jovial host!

If the day ever comes when I cannot physically run this business to the standard I want, I hope that my son's kids will be far enough along in their school-life so that he and his wife can follow me to this sunny land, and take over the day-to-day running of the house. Dino is keen to make his mark here, eventually, and he accepts that The Old Man will be sitting there in the corner, nodding and smiling and chatting with anyone who has the time to share "une verre" and a tale or two. Those days are not with us yet, however. I have only taken sixty-seven turns around this planet and I intend to take many more. The positive energy of listening to my heart and following my dream gives a spring to my step and I have so many plans and schemes still to fulfill … Everyone needs Projects!

And now, here's my final reminder:

CHAPTER 15.

SAY
"THANK YOU"

Say "Thank You" – to everyone

One fundamental essential, if you want to really enjoy following your dream, whatever it might be, is to never stop saying "Thank You".

You can be forgiven for thinking that you are the Brightest Shining Star in your Universe – having worked so hard, assumed every role, and made a success of your uniquely personal B&B business. You are, most definitely, The Key Player, but as my favourite Canadian friend and mentor says "It's teamwork that makes the dream work"… in all the nicest ways.

So …

Say Thank You to the mason for making the walls;

Say Thank You to the translator for explaining the words;

Say Thank You to your best friend for being such a multi-tasking, always-there, never-fail best friend;

Say Thank You to everyone for their contributions along the way;

Say Thank You to all those who have called

by to share the good times, and the tough times, together;

Say Thank You to the musicians who make others sing and who make you dance;

Say Thank You to yourself, for all that you are, all that you've done and all that you continue to be.

And, finally, I say "Thank You" most wholeheartedly to my Girlfriend … for showing up on my doorstep, and for writing this book.

MY LIST OF CONTACTS AND CONNECTIONS

Air Conditioning: Dakin are a high-quality brand and their units run very quietly.

https://www.polarpumpen.se/varmepumpar/luftvarmepump/luft-luft-varmepump/daikin-daikin-m3-r-luftvarmepump/p-1224278

Beds. The Best, in my opinion, are Carpe Diem beds. Made in Sweden.

https://carpediembeds.com/

Bed linen, towels, bathroom supplies and so much more.

https://bed-bath.com/hotellrum/

Electromagnetic Descaler, FLR-20 dissolves limescale. This little machine can save you lots of money and dramatically reduce any problems with limescale.

https://www.elgruvan.se/en/home-leisure/73-flr-20-descaler-electromagnetic-lime-solver-7350043310066.html

Ironing board. EOLO. The Ferrari of professional ironing boards, in my opinion!

https://www.amazon.de/-/en/EOLO-GV05-Professional-ironing-container/dp/B00W1UKK98/ref=sr_1_21?crid=24T3T4PV45Q5Y&keywords=professionelle+b%C3%BCgelstation+-+dampfgenerator&qid=1656695107&sprefix=professional+ironing+station+-+steam+generator+%2Caps%2C68&sr=8-21

Washing machines and dryers. Refurbished. Call and ask to speak with Henrick …

https://www.httvattmaskiner.se

Website. Elloha. A fantastic platform for your website and reservations system, easy to use and with the ability to translate to different languages too. Brilliant!

www.elloha.com

And finally, they are not everyone's favourite company, but shopping on Amazon (especially Amazon.de for Europe) can save you a lot of time and money ~

We found this amazing new addition to our cleaning "staff" recently; we call him Fritz and he's a Robot. He's doing a great job sweeping every room every day and saving me hours of work. I  don't know how I ever managed without him. He's one "employee" I'm happy to keep; he's so quiet, so helpful and so good. Buy yourself one … straight away!

https://www.amazon.fr/gp/product/B09SP4FJ6H/ref=ppx_yo_dt_b_asin_image_o02_s00?ie=UTF8&psc=1

HOW IT ALL BEGAN

We've come a long way

OTHER TITLES FOR YOU TO ENJOY:

Brave or Stupid

Janne and Carl's true story of how two middle-aged seasick electricians sailed around the World on a three-year voyage that would change them forever.

Written by Tracey Christiansen
www.braveorstupid.com

Dream It, Do It ... Why not?

Sara's true story of moving, alone, from her buzzing seaside home in Brighton to a village in a valley in the hills of rural France, where tractors out-number the residents 2 to 1.

Written by Sara Verrall
www.dreamitdoit.fr

Sara Verrall

The Author

Lightning Source UK Ltd.
Milton Keynes UK
UKHW022201090922
408613UK00007B/744